for middle-age children

Norma Stevens

Family Touch.

Nashville, Tennessee

7806-43
ISBN: 0-8054-9966-0

Dewey Decimal Classification: 155.3
Subject Heading: SEX EDUCATION//SEXUAL BEHAVIOR
Printed in the United States of America

Scripture quotations marked NIV are from the Holy Bible, New
International Version, copyright © 1973, 1978, 1984 by International
Bible Society.
Scripture quotations marked RSV are from the Revised Standard
Version of the Bible, copyrighted 1946, 1952, © 1971, 1973.

Family Touch Press
127 Ninth Avenue, North
Nashville, TN 37234

My Body and Me

A Look at Me

What would you say if someone asked, "What are you?"

Would you reply, "I am a child"?

Then they might ask, "Are there others like you?" Would you answer, "Yes" or "No?" The answer is both yes and no. Yes, there are many other children like you. God made all people in His image. No, there is no other child exactly like you. God made people to be one-of-a-kind.

God said, Let us make man in our image, in our likeness. . . and it was very good (Genesis 1:26,31, NIV).

You might want to believe you are like everyone else you know or you may like the idea of being different.

Think about giraffes. Once you have seen one giraffe, you can identify a giraffe whenever you see one. However, no two giraffes have the same number of spots in exactly the same places. Giraffes are not all the same in color. Each giraffe is a slightly different shape from all other giraffes. Yet, a giraffe is a giraffe and you can describe or maybe even draw a giraffe.

You, of course, are not a giraffe. You are a human being made in the image of God. The Bible tells us human beings are the most special of all God's creation. How are you like other human beings? As a human being you can recognize other human beings when you see them. They have two legs, two arms, two eyes, and two ears. While you may know some human beings who do not have two eyes or two arms, you can still recognize they are humans and not giraffes. In those ways you are like other human beings. And you are like other human beings in that you can depend on God to help you make your choices.

When you think of yourself as a person made in God's image, you can begin to see how you are one-of-a-kind. Even if you are a twin, you received **genes**. (When you see words highlighted like this, look them up in the glossary in the back of the book.) Genes make you different from anyone else in the world. Genes are tiny carriers of all the things you are. They determine your particular physical features— how tall you will be when you grow up, the color of your eyes and hair. Even your fingerprints are different. Did you ever hear somebody say you had your father's eyes or your uncle's nose? When you were little, did you think they meant you really had taken those eyes or that nose from the other person? Then you looked at your father and he still had his eyes and it did not make sense. *Having your father's eyes* means the genes you received from your father caused you to have the same shape or color eyes as your father. But how would you get your nose from an uncle? Just as your genes came from your parents, your parent's genes came from their parents. So, you can have genes for a nose like an uncle, a smile like a grandmother, eyes like your father, and hair like your mother. **Physically** you are like other human beings. And at the same time, you are one-of-a-kind—you are you. God made you special.

AND THAT IS GOOD!

You have a body similar to everyone else in the world. The body of a human being. You have a body that is growing and changing and that has one-of-a-kind features. You do not look the same as you did as a baby. You are growing physically. Look at one of your baby pictures to see how much you have changed.

You may be short or tall, skinny or chubby. You may have pale skin or dark skin, long or short hair. You may have freckles or you may tan easily. The important thing is that you are you and God made you the way you are.

AND THAT IS GOOD

You are growing **spiritually**. God gave people the ability to grow spiritually. You are like others in that you have the God-given ability to know God and to be aware of things related to Him. You are different from others in that you are growing spiritually in your own way.

You may often think about God and what He wants you to do. You may think about being the kind of person God would have you to be. You probably have a lot of questions about God at this time in your life. It is hard to understand a lot of things about God. You can read the Bible and know God loves you and that He created you in His image.

AND THAT IS VERY GOOD!

God gave you a mind. You can think and figure out things. You are growing mentally. You know many more things than you did even a few months ago. You want to know a lot more about a lot of different things. You have already had many kinds of experiences. You have gone places and seen things and you know a lot about the world. You are like some others your age. But, everyone is different.

AND THAT IS GOOD!

You are growing in the way you feel—**emotionally**. Do you remember when you used to cry when someone took a toy away from you? You do not cry so easily now. Now your crying is because you are hurt physically or emotionally, and not just because you are angry at not having something or not getting your way. You probably know a friend or two who are different from you. They may not have learned how to handle their emotions yet. You may have times when you cannot handle your emotions. The Bible says, "Rejoice with those who rejoice; weep with those who weep" (Romans 12:15, RSV). So, you can be sad when your friends are upset and happy when they are happy.

AND THAT IS GOOD!

You are growing **socially**. You usually remember to tell people "Thank you," or to say "Excuse me," and that shows how much you are growing socially. You may even go out to a special dinner with your parents or spend the night with friends all by yourself. You know people who live in your part of town, those who go to your church, and the parents of your school friends. Your world is getting bigger and you know how to act in that world.

AND THAT IS GOOD!

You are growing! Do you ever look at your friends and wish you were as tall as one or had curly hair like another? Sometimes you may think you would rather have another hair color. Perhaps everyone wishes he or she were a little different. The wonderful thing about YOU is that you are exactly right for you. You are growing and changing just as God planned. And it's OK to like yourself. You are just what you need to be right now. You are just as big as you need to be. You look just like you need to look.

AND THAT IS GOOD!

You are old enough to begin to know what you like and what you don't like. You may be aware that one friend likes all kinds of vegetables and another one won't eat any vegetables but potatoes. Each person develops likes and dislikes. You know what kind of ice cream you order. You know which games you like to play. You have developed likes and dislikes that go together to make you YOU.

Each person also develops certain abilities as he or she grows. You may be able to hop on one foot and whistle at the same time, tell interesting stories, or play a musical instrument. Whatever you do, YOU do it slightly differently from the way anyone else does it.

Think about the things you like and the abilities God has given you. Think how you feel about yourself when others listen to you. Think how you feel about yourself when you do a job or play a game really well. It is important that you feel good about YOU.

We started out talking about how you are both alike and different from other people. You have now determined that not everyone is alike and that the differences are usually good. You know from experience it is fun to get to know all kinds of people. An important part of your growing is in the area of getting along with other people. You make friends by being friendly and helpful to other people and by letting them be helpful to you.

It is important to feel good about yourself. You have to feel good about yourself before you can feel good about other people. You feel good about yourself when you help another person get something done. You also feel good when another person helps you get something done. You feel good about yourself when you do what you have promised to do. When you say good night to your parents, you can feel good about yourself if you have taken your responsibilities seriously.

You can feel good about yourself when you have been honest with your brother or sister.

You can feel good when you have been a friend to a new child in your school. Remember this: how you act toward other people is a major part of who YOU are. You will have no trouble liking yourself if you treat others as you want to be treated. God says we should do to others

as we would have them do to us (Luke 6:31).
  God told us to love other people as we love
ourselves. So you have friends whom you like
and love and who like and love you.

AND THAT IS GOOD!

What's Happening to Me?

Would the person who asked what you are be able to identify you if he saw a picture taken when you were two years old? Maybe not! You have changed! And you are still changing. You are probably growing about two or three inches and getting heavier by three to six pounds each year. Your muscles are still developing.

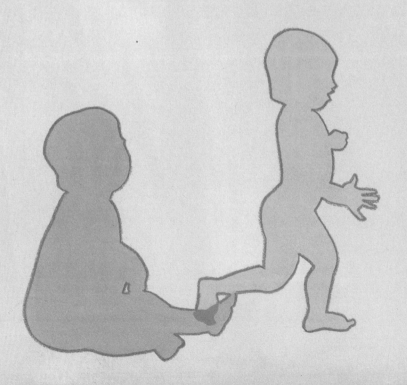

You are able to do a lot of things you couldn't do when you were five or six years old.

You may have freckles now that you didn't have a year ago. Your hair may stick out in ways it hasn't done before. You may bump into things or knock things over because your legs and arms may not always go the way you mean them to go. You are still growing.

AND THAT IS GOOD!

You like to talk and usually enjoy reading. You enjoy jokes and funny stories. You don't need to take naps as you did when you were younger. You have a lot of energy and a lot of different things interest you. You are trying to

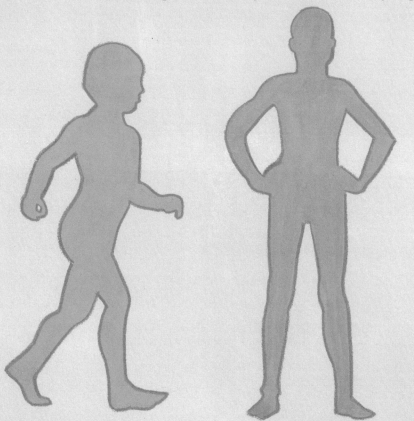

be honest and truthful. You are attempting to be responsible for the things your parents and teachers want you to do. You may not always understand what it is adults want you to do. Still, you understand a lot more than you did when you were younger. And you are learning new things every day.

AND THAT IS GOOD!

If someone asked you, "Are you a boy or girl?" you wouldn't have any trouble answering. If you are a girl, you know you are different from a boy; and if you are a boy you know you are different from a girl. God made boys and girls to be different. Sometimes these differences are the ones that cause some embarrassment. If you were to go into the wrong rest room at school or at church, it would probably embarrass you. You are learning what is acceptable to other people and what is not. You are also learning about **modesty** in connection with your body. It is modest behavior to close the door when you go to the bathroom and not to dress or undress in front of others.

Sometimes your body surprises you by doing things you wish it wouldn't do in public. This happens to everyone and often children your age laugh when someone burps loudly or makes other body noises. This is funny when it

16

happens to someone else but not so funny when it happens to you. You are learning not to make fun of other people. You are learning, when it happens to you, say, "Excuse me," and to go on with what you were doing.

The physical changes that are happening to you are fascinating and sometimes confusing and scary.

STAY OUT!

As you are getting older you are developing in all kinds of new ways. You are discovering a part of something called human sexuality. Human **sexuality** has to do with certain portions of your body, with certain feelings, and with certain responsibilities you have in relationship to other people. And God planned it that way.

AND THAT IS GOOD!

God has given husbands and wives the ability to love each other in a special way. It is this special way of loving that allows husbands and wives to have children. God planned for that in the beginning with Adam and Eve. The parts of the body that allow the miracle of birth to take place, develop very slowly over a long period of time. You are developing some of those parts now. Your body has a lot of growing to do. Your have a lot to learn about your body and how God wants you to take care of it.

AND THAT IS GOOD!

You are also learning about how important other people are to you. You know how your parents take care of you. You know how much they love you by the way they treat you. Your parents may tell you to go to bed at a certain time on school nights. They may tell you certain foods are good for you. They may not let you eat some foods that are not good for you. Your parents have been through the same growth changes you are going through. They have learned, as you are learning, that loving others means you sometimes say no. They have learned from the Bible that loving and caring for others is based on caring enough to do what is best for the others and yourself.

You are learning that although you do not always want to do what your parents tell you to do, you need to obey them. You are also learning that the way you react to your responsibilities and to family rules makes a difference in how pleasant or unpleasant life in your home can be. You are learning that you have a responsibility to be fair and honest with family members. You may be finding out that you can claim some space and some belongings for just you. Have you noticed that when you let others have a place to be alone (**privacy**), you often get to have your own place to be alone? You may be finding out that your smaller brother or sister has not learned this lesson yet. If that is so, you are having to learn to be patient. You may also be learning how to help that brother or sister learn about privacy.

Do to others as you would have them do to

you. (Luke 6:31, NIV)

Remember the idea of treating others as you would like to be treated? You have a great place to practice that rule in your own home. You can feel good about who you are, if you will always treat others fairly. Feeling good about yourself means knowing you acted in a way that was pleasing to God. It means you know you will try to be fair. You do not always have to get your way. It means that sometimes to have what you want, you are willing to wait (be patient) and willing to share.

Be kind and compassionate to one another (Ephesians 4:32, NIV).

Think about some of the things that make you feel good about yourself. Maybe you feel good about yourself when your parents tell you they are proud of you or of something you do. Or maybe you feel good about yourself when you do something all by yourself and it turns out well. And maybe you feel good about yourself when your teacher lets you do something important. It is true, you will feel good when you please other people and they let you know it by praising you. You will feel good when you play a game of ball well or when you win a game. Those experiences are important, but the good feelings only last until you have to perform again. Then, what happens if you do

not make a good grade or if you lose the game?
You will not get the praise. You may feel bad
about yourself.

AND THAT IS NOT SO GOOD!

You have heard, God is love. It is God's loving plan for you to learn to love yourself and others. His plan for you began with your parents' love for each other. His plan has given to husbands and wives that special way to love each other that allows children to be born. God said that marriage is good. He said that husbands and wives should love each other and, in that love, may have children. God is love. He loves you. He gave you a sexual identity. If you are a boy, your sexual identity is male like your father. If you are a girl, your sexual identity is female like your mother.

The changes in your body that are taking place are part of God's plan for your sexual identity. You are becoming an adult. You have your parents and other adults to help you understand your sexual identity and how to understand others.

AND THAT IS GOOD!

What's Happening to Others?

You have read about how you are different from others. You have learned you are one-of-a-kind.

Now, think about families. Your family is like other families; your family is different from other families; and your family is one-of-a-kind. Just as there is no one else exactly like you, there is no other family exactly like your family.

AND THAT IS GOOD!

Some families have six children and two parents. Some families have no children and some families have one child and one parent. Some families are made up of a grandfather, a grandmother, and grandchildren. Some families have lots of relatives who live nearby. Some families have no relatives who live in the same country in which the family lives.

Each family has its customs and routines. Families may celebrate birthdays and holidays with parties or they may not celebrate at all. Families may or may not worship together. Families who do worship together may go to church to worship.

You may have noticed when you have stayed overnight with a friend that her/his family does things differently. Perhaps you like the way your friend's family does one thing and you like the way your family does other things.

One thing all families have in common is

that the people in the families need some place they can go for a time and not be disturbed, even if it is only the bathroom.

Think now, about your own family. You know who wants to be left alone in the morning. You know how much noise you can make before your parents will ask you to be quiet. You have probably figured out by now that sometimes

your mother wants to be alone and sometimes
your father wants to be alone. Or they may
choose to be alone together. You may not
understand why that is so. You may have an
older sister or brother who does not want you
in his or her room. That brother or sister is
growing and changing just as you are going to
grow and change. One of the changes that

may be happening to your older brother or sister is that he or she is growing **pubic hair** and hair under his or her arms. It is important for you to know that these changes are going to happen and why. Whether you are a girl or a boy, you need to know you will change and how a person of the opposite **sex** will change.

Your body is changing to prepare you for the possibility of having children when you marry. God planned it that way.

AND THAT IS GOOD!

Girls, about your age or a little older, are experiencing growth of their breasts. Breasts are God's way for mothers to feed newborn babies. Girls have parts that are developing inside their bodies. These parts are the **ovaries** and the **uterus**. The ovaries produce eggs. The uterus is where a baby grows from a **fertilized** egg. When the ovaries develop, a girl may have her **menstrual** period. When the ovaries send an egg to the uterus and the egg is not fertilized, the uterus sheds its lining. This is called a menstrual period and happens each month. This lining is a bloody discharge that comes out the **vagina**. For some of this time each month (five to seven days), a girl may want more privacy than at other times.

AND THAT IS GOOD!

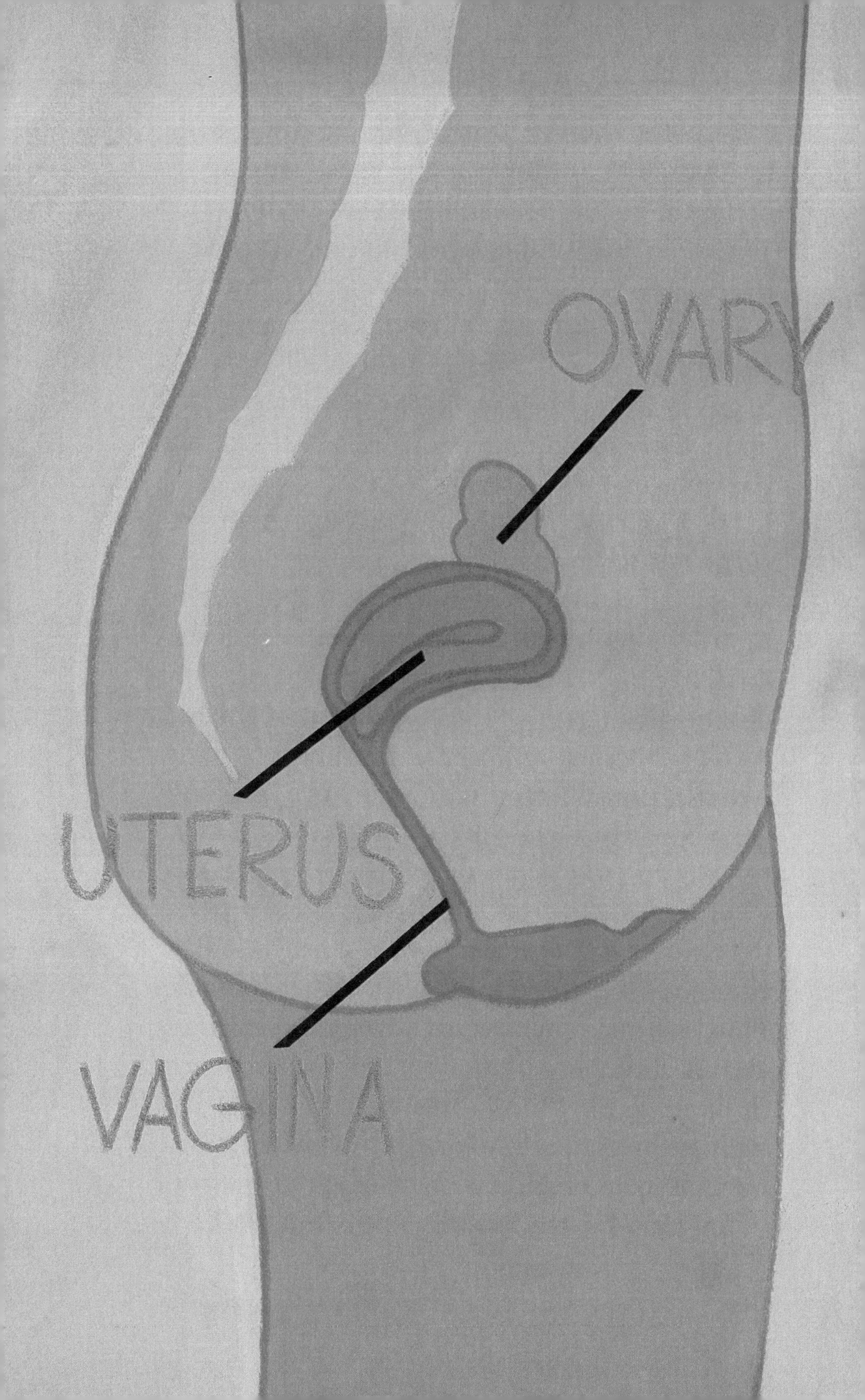
OVARY
UTERUS
VAGINA

Boys your age or a little older are beginning to develop to prepare for the possibility of being the father of a child when they marry. Their body parts that are changing are the **penis**, the **testicles**, and **scrotum**. The scrotum is a soft bag under the penis which contains the testicles. As they get older, boys begin to have erections of the penis more often. This means the penis gets stiff and bigger than usual.

The testicles produce **sperm**. Sperm are tiny cells that look like tadpoles that cannot be seen with the eye. When a woman's egg and a man's sperm meet, the egg is said to be fertilized. Sperm are carried in a fluid called **semen** through the erect penis out of the body. As they begin to change, boys sometimes have a discharge of semen while they are sleeping. This is because they are growing up.
AND THAT IS GOOD!

This physical growth happens at the right time for each person. Some of these changes may be happening to you now. Some of these changes may not happen to you for two, three, or more years. When the changes happen, it will be the right time for you. In time you will be more comfortable with the changes.

You may have a friend your own age who is

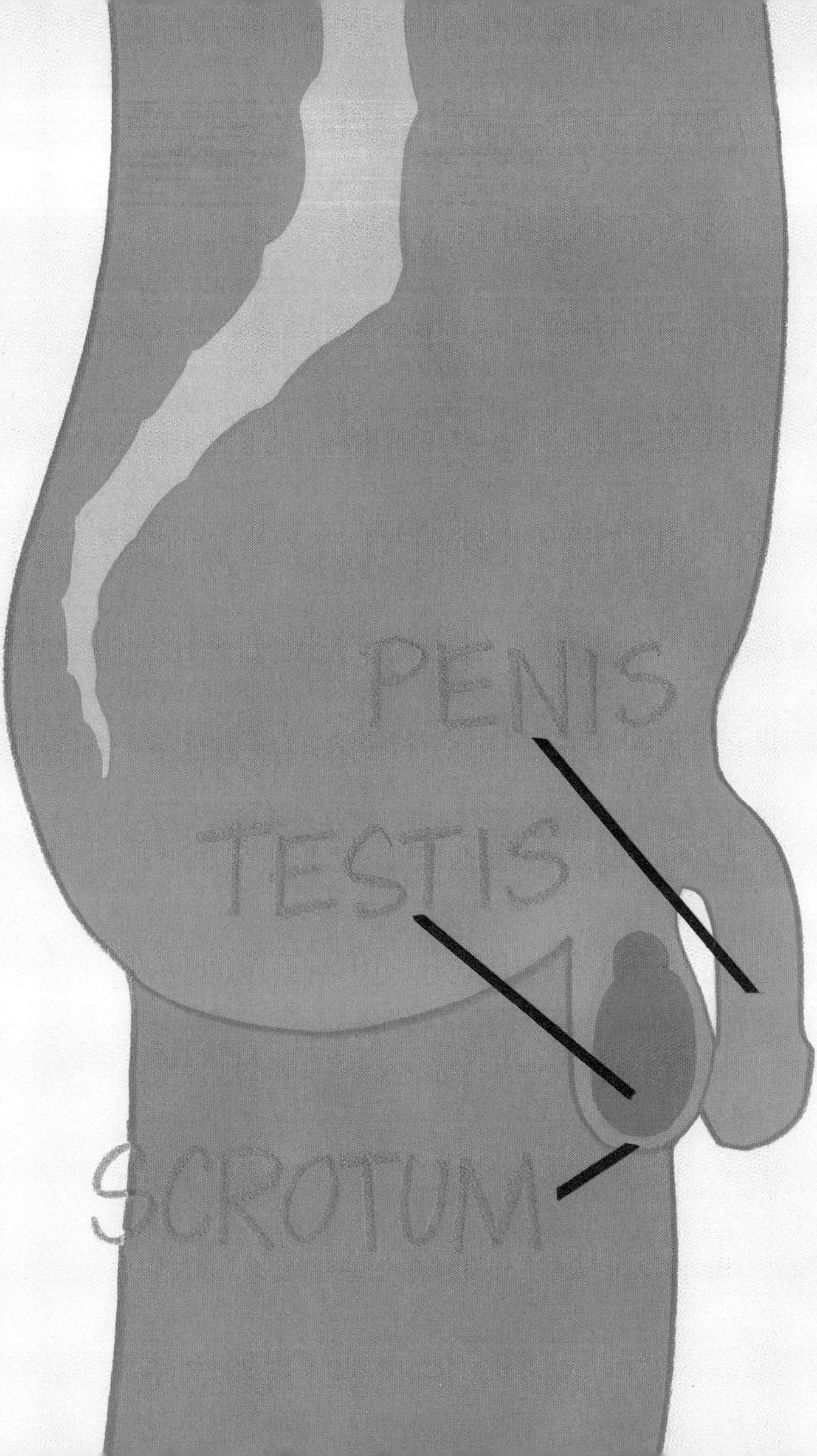
PENIS
TESTIS
SCROTUM

maturing faster than you. You may be the one who is maturing faster than your friend. If your friend is maturing faster than you, you may wonder if something is wrong with you or your friend. Your friend may be shy about the changes that are taking place. This is a time for you to be understanding about your friend's feelings. You need to understand your own feelings, too. We do not all grow at the same rate. You and your friends are growing at the rate that each of you should grow.

As a boy or girl, you grow fast between the second and fifth grades. You get taller and larger. You develop the ability to do a lot of things you could not do before. You are capable of reading more difficult books. You can print better. You learn how to write cursive. You learn how to talk to people. You learn how to be responsible for pets, your room, and your belongings. You may still feel small sometimes.

You have grown a lot, but you are still growing. This is all part of God's plan.

AND THAT IS GOOD!

I Am Special to God

You are special to many people. You are special to God. You are special to God because He created you. He created you to live according to His plan. God knows everything about you. God knows the number of hairs on your head.

The very hairs of your head are all numbered (Luke 12:7, NIV).

You are one-of-a-kind and that means no one can take your place. God knows how you are, what you are, and where you are each moment of your life. You are very, very special to Him.
AND THAT IS VERY, VERY GOOD!

God wants you to have a good life. He wants you to be able to do all of the things He would have you to do. When you were a baby, you gurgled and crawled from one side of the room to the other. When you were a toddler, you were able to jump up and down and to throw a ball. As a five- or six-year-old you learned to print your name and to read. Each year as you have gotten older, you know more and you can do more things. God's plan for you is that you grow to be all you can be.

Your body is part of God's plan for you. It is important that you understand your body. It is good for you to know the correct names for the parts of your body. It is good for you to know what each part of your body does.

It may not be easy for you to realize that one day you might be a father (if you are a boy) or a mother (if you are a girl). You have a lot of growing and learning to do before that time, but your body is getting ready even now. The changes in your body are taking place so that, someday, you can be the mother or the father of children.

An important reason for you to learn about your body is to help you to follow God's perfect plan for your life. His plan is that you be prepared to take care of the children you may have. You need to know about your body and

understand what it means to be a boy who will become a man or to be a girl who will become a woman.

If you do not know and understand the importance of sexuality (being a male or female), it is possible that you might become the mother or the father of a baby before you are ready. Sometimes babies are born to young people who have not done all of their growing and learning. And sometimes babies are born to adults who are not married. It is sad when God's perfect plan is not followed. It is easier for a baby to grow and feel good about himself

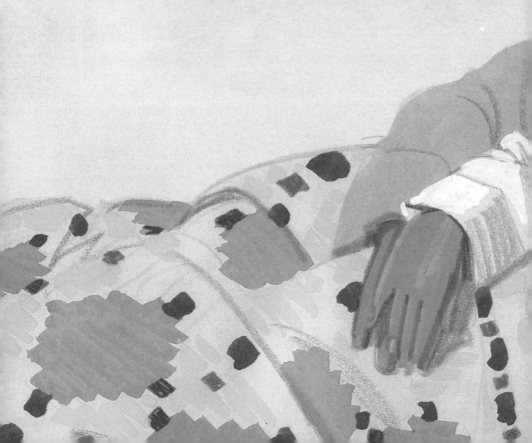

if he has a mother and a father who love each other and who love him.

Sex is God's special gift to husbands and wives. It is a special way to show love. God wants this special way of showing love to happen only after marriage.

AND THAT IS GOOD!

A husband and wife sleep in the same bed and usually show their special love for each other there because it is comfortable and private.

When the husband and wife are lying close to each other and they want to show their love for each other, the husband places his penis into the wife's vagina. This is a very loving act, the closest two people can ever get to each other. That is why God created this special enjoyment just for people who are married to each other.

For this reason a man will leave his father and mother and will be united to his wife, and they will become one flesh (Genesis 2:24).

During this loving act, semen comes from the end of the man's penis and goes into the woman's vagina. Semen is the name of a liquid made up of hundreds and thousands of sperm. Sperm are so tiny you can see them only under a microscope.

The sperm make their way through the woman's vagina, looking for an egg that the woman's ovaries release each month. If a sperm and an egg come together, fertilization takes place.

If during this sharing of love a fertilized egg finds its way down to the uterus in the woman and attaches itself to the lining, a baby begins to develop. The uterus (also called the womb) is a warm, dark place, full of liquid in which the baby floats while it grows for nine months. The mother's body feeds the baby through the

umbilical cord. From the outside it looks like the mother's stomach is getter bigger and bigger. Actually the baby is growing in the uterus, not the stomach. After a few months, if you put your hand on the mother's stomach, you might even feel the baby kicking.

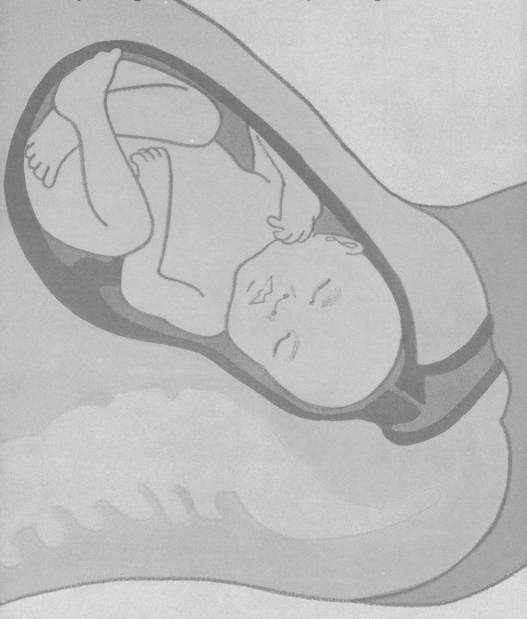

At the same time the baby is growing inside the mother's body, the mother's breasts are being prepared to produce milk. When the baby is born the mother will have milk in her breasts to feed the baby.

When the baby is finally large enough, the mother usually goes to a hospital where a doctor helps the baby to come out through the vagina. Then the baby starts breathing by itself. The umbilical cord that has connected the baby to the uterus is cut. Where the cord was cut when you were born is your navel.

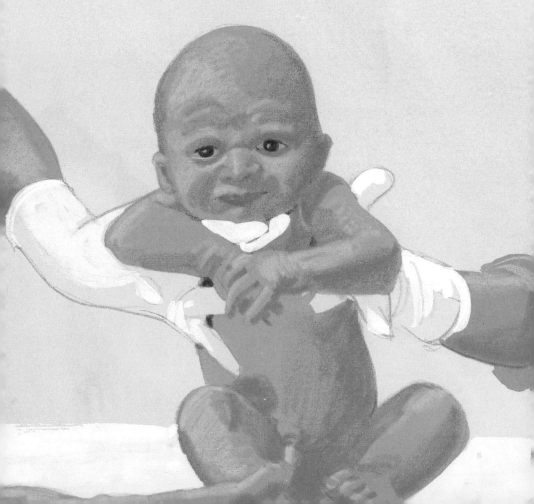

The newborn baby is totally helpless. Someone must take care of him or her. The mother often nurses (breast feeds) the baby. If the mother does not breast feed, the baby can have all of the same good nutrition from a formula. A formula is a mixture of several things that is a lot like the mother's milk and is fed to the baby from a bottle. However the baby is fed, she eats and sleeps and grows.

AND THAT IS GOOD!

Isn't it a miracle that God created people in such a way that two people can love each other so much and that they can have a baby? Isn't it wonderful to think about your mother and father loving each other and having you?

It is important that you know about you body. You need to know what the parts of your body are called. You are in the stage of growing right now before your body makes some major changes. Some children your age are very well developed physically and may already be using deodorant because of body odor. Some girls may be wearing bras because their breasts are growing. These changes are signs that you are growing up.

AND THAT IS GOOD!

At this time in your life you are not ready to get married and be a parent. Sometimes children are pressured into having sexual **intercourse** just to please another person. That can result in a baby. Intercourse may also be called "making love," or "having sex." It is wrong to have intercourse before marriage, and it displease God.

One of the most important things to remember in learning to protect yourself from people who might harm you and who do not know of God's perfect plan for you is to think about the friends you make. You know so many more people than you used to know. You probably have a lot of friends, and you will be making more in the next few years. Each day you are learning new and better ways to be friends. But you don't have to give anything away to have a friend. You don't have to bribe people with toys or money, and you don't have to do things that are not right for you.

So, if a friend wants you to play a game that you are uncomfortable about, just say, "I don't play that kind of game." If an adult touches you in places that make you uncomfortable, tell him or her not to do it and then tell someone—your parents or a teacher or the pastor of your church. Tell someone, even if you are threatened.

"What are you?" "Who are you?" Maybe after reading this book you can say "I am a boy , or girl who was created by God in His image. I am not like anybody else in the world. I am special to God. He has made me so that I can learn and grow and become what He would have me to be. Because God made me in His image, one day I can probably be the father, or mother, of a baby.

You can be glad you are different from everyone else. You can be glad you are like everyone else in all the important ways. You can be glad

God made each of us in His image. You can be glad God gave us the way by which adults can love each other and children can be born.
ALL OF THIS IS VERY, VERY GOOD!

Glossary

emotionally (i-moh-sho-nal-lee): how you feel. Joy, grief, fear, hate, love, anger, and excitement are emotions.

fertilized (fur-til-ized) egg: when a woman's egg and a man's sperm meet the egg is said to be fertilized.

gene (jeen): a tiny part of a chromosome (part of a cell) that influences the passing on of physical or mental characteristics from parent to child.

intercourse (in-ter-kohrs): sex between a man and a woman.

menstrual (men-stroo-al) period: when the ovaries send an egg to the uterus and the egg is not fertilized, the uterus sheds its lining producing a bloody discharge from the vagina.

mentally (men-tal-lee): things related to how you think and your ability to think.

modesty (mod-ist-ee): how you show respect for the privacy of others and yourself.

ovaries (oh-va-rees): the part of a woman's body that produces eggs.

penis (pee-nis): the male sex reproductive organ.

physically (fiz-i-kal-lee): things that relate to the growth and development of your body.

privacy (pri-va-see): the need to be alone or by oneself.

puberty (pu-ber-ti): the time of becoming first capable of reproducing sexually.

pubic hair (pu-bic hair): the body hair that appears on the lower part of the abdomen region at puberty.

scrotum (skroh-tum): the pouch that contains the testicles of a man.

semen (see-men): fluid containing the male reproductive cells.

sex (seks): being male or female. Also a term used to describe a male and female making love or having intercourse.

sexuality (sek-shoo-al-i-tee): the difference between being a male or female—boy or girl.

socially (soh-shal-lee): how you relate to other people. Being kind, courteous, and helpful are socially acceptable traits.

sperm (spurm): tiny male reproductive cells that look like tadpoles.

spiritually (spir-i-choo-al-lee): caring for things related to God and the church.

testicles (tes-ti-kels): the gland in a man that produces sperm.

umbilical (um-bil-i-kal) cord: the cord that carries food to the baby and waste from the baby while it is growing inside the uterus.

uterus (yoo-te-rus): the part of a woman's body that holds and feeds a baby until it is born.

vagina (va-ji-na): the passage way inside a woman that leads from the uterus to the outside of her body.